James Otis

When Israel Putnam served the King

James Otis

When Israel Putnam served the King

ISBN/EAN: 9783743348219

Manufactured in Europe, USA, Canada, Australia, Japa

Cover: Foto ©ninafisch / pixelio.de

Manufactured and distributed by brebook publishing software (www.brebook.com)

James Otis

When Israel Putnam served the King

WHEN ISRAEL PUTNAM SERVED THE KING

BY

JAMES OTIS

AUTHOR OF "JENNY WREN'S BOARDING-HOUSE," "JERRY'S FAMILY,"
"THE BOYS' REVOLT," "THE BOYS OF 1745," ETC.

Illustrated

BOSTON
ESTES AND LAURIAT
1898

CONTENTS.

CHAPTER		PAGE
	NOTE	11
I.	AT SOUTH BAY	15
II.	THE ATTACK	32
III.	DESERTING THE WOUNDED	50
IV.	SEWATIS	65
V.	NEAR FORT ANNE	81
VI.	THE PRISONER	97

LIST OF ILLUSTRATIONS.

	PAGE
"The Indian bound Israel Putnam hand and foot to a tree" . . . . . . *Frontispiece*	
Old Seabury telling the young soldier the story .	12
"'Glad to see you, young Seabury'" . . .	19
Building the breastworks	24
Awaiting the enemy	29
The arrival of the enemy	37
"'We'll stand back to back'"	43
A volley of musketry from the foliage . .	47
In the wilderness	57
The two cowards	62
Sewatis bound to a tree	71
"We dashed forward"	76
In camp near Fort Anne	83
"Major Rogers was skulking in the rear" . .	93
Sewatis finds the trail	101
Molang in the uniform of a French officer . .	107

"Tell me if you can," the boy asked, after reading the lines, "tell me if you can, in what way the King's troops in 1755 excelled those who have just been discharged from service."

"That will best be done by relating to you the part Amos Cowden and I played under Major Israel Putnam in 1758, nearabout Lake Champlain; and when the story is finished, if it so be you care to hear it, I will leave you to say whether we who fought then, in the wilderness, with inferior weapons, each man for himself as it were, did not make a better showing than you who are so lately returned full of boasting."

What may have followed between the old and the young soldier after this conversation is not known; but on the next page of manuscript, in very nearly the same words here used, appears the tale told by Zenas Seabury.

WHEN ISRAEL PUTNAM SERVED THE KING.

NOTE.

THIS tale is rewritten from a time-worn manuscript, very nearly as there set down by a lad seventeen years of age, who served his country during the War of 1812.

It was within a few months after having been honourably discharged from the service (probably in 1815) that the writer, Enoch Wilson, met one Captain Zenas Seabury, an old man nearly eighty years of age, who repeated the substance of this story, to prove to the boy so lately from the second conflict with the mother country, that in the olden times "soldiers were soldiers, and not make-believes."

From Enoch's written statement, it would appear that he took umbrage at this remark, and loudly maintained that the troops who answered to their country's call in 1812 were better soldiers in every way than any who had then been seen on this side the Atlantic Ocean, not excepting those sent over in 1776 by King George to bring the unruly colonists into subjection.

"To prove that you are mistaken, I will tell of what we did, Amos Cowden and I, when Israel Putnam served the King," the old man said, boastfully, and the boy asked, sceptically:

"Do you mean *our* General Putnam?"

"Aye, lad, that I do, although he was major when I enlisted under him."

"But he never served the King!"

"Think you so, lad? Then, since you are through playing the soldier, it is time you read more concerning the history of those men who, by their deeds of valour, purchased for you this country, whose dignity you have been doing your little part towards sustaining. In 1755, when what is known as the French War was in progress, Israel Putnam tilled the soil like many another good man before him, in the settlement of Pomfret, over Connecticut way.

He was appointed to command the first troops raised in that vicinity, and given a major's commission. Now, hark you, lad, it was the King's commission, not one from Continental Congress, that our General Putnam first held. I am not minded to make any long story of what he has done for this land which we now call the United States, because, perchance, there are not sufficient years of mine in this world remaining in which to tell it. The lines inscribed on a slab in the graveyard at Brooklyn, in the State of Connecticut, sum up all he was, and I have writ it down."

The old soldier took from his pocket a slip of paper, which he handed the boy, and on it was the epitaph of the officer under whom he had served.

It read as follows:

This monument is erected to the memory of the Honourable Israel Putnam, Esq., major-general in the armies of the United States of America, who was born at Salem, in the Province of Massachusetts, on the seventh day of January, 1718, and died at Brooklyn, in the State of Connecticut, on the twenty-ninth day of May, A. D. 1790. Passenger, if thou art a soldier, go not away till thou hast dropped a tear over the dust of a Hero, who, ever tenderly attentive to the lives and happiness of his men, dared to lead where any one dared to follow. If thou art a patriot, remember with gratitude how much thou and thy country owe to the disinterested and gallant exertions of the patriot who sleeps beneath this marble. If thou art an honest, generous, and worthy man, render a sincere and cheerful tribute of respect to a man whose generosity was singular; whose honesty was proverbial; and who, with a slender education, with small advantages, and without powerful friends, raised himself to universal esteem, and to offices of eminent distinction, by personal worth, and by the diligent services of a useful life.

CHAPTER I.

AT SOUTH BAY.

IT was in June of 1758 when Amos Cowden and I, living nearabout Pomfret, in Connecticut, decided that the time had come when we should serve the King, providing it might be done under the command of Major Israel Putnam, whom we well knew to be a brave man and a good soldier.

Amos was little more than fourteen, — I within two months of being fifteen; but boys in those days were older at that age than they seem now to be at one and twenty.

We were not wholly inexperienced in such warfare as the French were then carrying on, for the Indian war-whoop had been heard by both of us many a time, and more than once had we followed our elders against the savages in order to the better secure safety for our homes.

Of that time, when he who went abroad must perforce carry his musket with him, as the lads of this day do their walking-sticks, it is not necessary I should make many words, for you already know how we who plunged into the wilderness to find a homestead, fought against beasts and savages to maintain a foothold.

Nor shall I explain all that Amos and I did in the way of preparing for a soldier's life.

We who fought then provided our own uniforms, — which were neither more nor less than the clothes we hunted in, — our own weapons, and more often our own ammunition.

It is enough when I say we were bent on offering our services to Major Putnam, and knew that his command was at Fort Edward, under General Abercrombie.

To make our way from Connecticut to Lake Champlain was not looked upon as any very great hardship, although I question if you find many lads to-day, fourteen or fifteen years old, who would willingly set out through the forest on such a tramp.

We had made up our minds to go, and we went, arriving at our destination in reasonably good season.

The major seemed glad to see us, and well he might, for recruits who could be depended upon to stand against the savage bands, which the French had made a pretence of enlisting, were not to be found in considerable numbers.

Although I say it who should not, and while there is no thought in my mind of disparaging the English soldiers under General Abercrombie, I am free to declare that a lad like Amos Cowden or myself, in such work as was needed at the time, stood fully the equal of any three redcoats to be found at Fort Edward.

As a matter of course, when it came to fighting according to rule, we made a precious poor showing, not because there was any lack of courage, but owing to our not understanding the drill.

To those in the forest, however, where no enemy is to be seen, and yet a murderous fire is poured upon one from every side, as I said before, we were equal to three, yes, to ten trained soldiers who knew no more than to stand up and be shot at.

As for beating the redcoats at their own game, why, bless you, lad, they were like teething babies, and fell by the score where not a single life need have been lost.

Afterward, we who fought side by side with them in '58 showed that, with a bit of training, we could stand equally well in front of them in '76, and, what is more, we did it, to their sorrow.

However, that is neither here nor there, so far as telling you of the time when Israel Putnam served the King.

As I said, we were come to Fort Edward and met the major.

There wasn't any red-tape business about calling out a recruiting officer and enlisting a man, swearing him in, and all that sort of folderol; but the major made soldiers of us a good deal like this:

"Glad to see you, young Seabury. How's your father? Has he been doing anything with winter wheat on that burnt land this year? Well, Cowden, you have decided it's time to serve the King, eh? Better that than trying to raise wool up Connecticut way. Enlist with me? Why, who else would a Pomfret boy serve under, if not Israel Putnam? Find yourselves quarters, and I'll see you have work in plenty. That red beast of a Molang is making it warm for us whenever he gets a chance, and you won't be idle."

We found quarters without much trouble, for a good many Pomfret lads served under the major, and before having been at the fort half an hour it was as if we were at home.

Now I am not counting on telling you all the whys and wherefores of the French wars, nor of the bloody business the frog-eaters daubed their hands in for the sake of besting us. It is only of the part Amos Cowden and I played, and we set about it in less than four and twenty hours from the time of having declared our willingness to serve the King.

When we arrived, Amos and I, General Abercrombie had already given commands that the Rangers — meaning in that case mostly the colonists who had enlisted like ourselves — were to set out from Fort Edward to watch the enemy nearabout Ticonderoga; for it was from that direction, as you know, that trouble might be expected, and it was from there that it did finally come.

Unused as I was to seeing large bodies of men together, it was difficult for me to guess just how many did march on that day after we came into the fort. To the best of my belief, however, there were between four and five hundred, in three divisions; the right under Major Rogers, the left, in which could be found Amos and I, under Major Putnam, and the centre under Captain Dalyell.

Now, in our division was, all told, not more than fifty,

and when, at the end of the second day's travel, we were arrived near to South Bay, on Lake Champlain, it was decided that Israel Putnam's force should remain there, while Major Rogers and Captain Dalyell were to go further on.

Why it was the troops did not keep together, I cannot say, unless the leaders had an idea that the redskins might make an approach from Lake George, at Bluff or Shelving Rock, after our people had gone on towards Ticonderoga.

However it might be, we camped at what was known as the Elbow, half a mile or less from the entrance to South Bay, and here it seemed to me at the time as if a great disaster came upon us, — one which could not well be explained.

The Rangers were a hardy set, like all the colonists in those days, and much averse to admitting that they were sick. I myself would have held my head up and marched with the command so long as it might be possible, however ill I felt, and you can fancy there was not a man among us inclined to be womanish.

Therefore it was, I say, a disaster which could not be explained, when more than half our force gave out entirely on the morning after making camp; and you may be certain not one among them was shamming.

The major danced here and there like a widow bewitched, trying to make up his mind what had so suddenly come over all hands, and knowing meanwhile, beyond any reasonable chance for doubt, that the brute of a Molang, with five, six, or seven hundred painted imps at his back, was prowling around close at hand.

Go back to the fort? Yes, of course we might; but I question, lad, whether Israel Putnam would have done such a thing even had the whole fifty of his men been unfit for duty.

As for Amos and I, we never so much as dreamed that such a thing could be possible.

It was a matter of pushing ahead, or, that being impossible, to remain where you were, rather than show up at the fort before the work mapped out had been performed.

If the major discovered what caused this sudden sickness, he did not tell us; but, on the second day, when the invalids showed little or no signs of improvement, fifteen were ordered back to the fort, and, although not a man of them but what should have been in the hospital, there was great ado made because Israel Putnam insisted they must beat a retreat.

However, to make a long story short, they went, and thirty-five of us remained on the lookout for Molang, giving little or no heed to the fact that we were but a handful of men waiting for the coming of hundreds.

Yes, I am free to admit it was not a pleasant outlook, particularly for Amos and I, who were green at this wholesale Injun-hunting, as you might call it; but perhaps both of us took good care to keep it a secret from each other if we grew timorous now and then, and when the squad of fifteen departed, grumbling furiously as they went, we who were left behind understood that we must do double duty if we would save our hair and our lives.

Our numbers were yet further reduced by the spies which the major kept on the move all the time, for, unlike the commander of the right division, who was not what you might call an Injun-fighter, Israel Putnam knew that, in measuring strength or cunning with Molang, he must ever be on the alert.

Now we all understood for a certainty that, when the savages made their appearance, it would be in such force that we could have but little chance against them, unless provided with something in the way of a fortification, and here was where the soldier in our major showed itself.

Near where we had camped, the lake, as you know, is very narrow, and the shores are like rocky cliffs, on the top of which are dense thickets.

We who were not on scouting duty, or acting as sentinels, were set about carrying loose rocks to the very edge of the cliffs, where we built a breastwork, as you might say, and afterwards, by hewing small pine-trees and placing them in front of this defence, completely hid it from view of any one who might pass on the lake.

It was such a fortification as heartened us all wonderfully, for even though we were determined to hold our own so long as might be, even Amos and I, the youngest of the party, knew full well of how little avail thirty-five men might be against such a force as Molang would bring. Therefore, I say, this breastwork heartened us wonderfully, and, at the close of the second day after the sick men of the division had left us, the major, making a tour of the little fort, halted in such a position that all might hear his words, saying cheerily, much as though inviting us to a feast at his own farmhouse in Pomfret :

"Lads, it is well done, and should serve better purpose than that of sheltering us while we lay here idle. If it so be you are minded, and I have a strong idea no one will say nay to the plan, we'll make an attack upon whatever force may come. Let that brute Molang show himself at the head of a hundred or a thousand, and I say to you, lads, we're a match for them. To pass down in canoes they must all come within musket-shot, and you are men who seldom waste a bullet. What say you?"

There was no cheering, for, situated as we were, even loud conversation was forbidden, and I believe no one before had raised his voice as high as our major when he thus addressed us.

Yet, if the cheers were lacking, the evidence of our spirit was not.

For reply to Israel Putnam's question, every one of us, and Amos and I were not among the hindermost, arose with our muskets in our hands, to show that we were ready for whatever might come.

If, perchance, there flashed into my mind the thought that, however brave a showing we might make when the red imps first appeared, there could be little question of the result should they give battle, it must not be set down as cowardice, for I hold to it that he only is brave who knows all the dangers before him.

"It is well," the major said, quietly, in a tone of content. "There is nothing now for us to do save remain on the alert. When a man among you sees a spot in the defence which might be strengthened, let him repair it, taking good heed, however, that the line is not weakened too severely, and from now until the red fiend Molang appears, if it so be he does, we must sleep with one eye open."

Bear in mind, lad, that we were but thirty-five. Within twenty miles at the farthest, and perhaps only a tenth of that distance away, was a force of French and Indians, so General Abercrombie had been informed, of not less than two thousand, and we had as leader a man who was of the mind to attack the first body of men or brutes which appeared, however large.

With that before you, you can, mayhap, understand

what was in Amos's mind and mine as, on this second night, we lay behind the wall of stones, listening intently for the slightest unusual sound, knowing it would betoken the coming of the foe.

"I am thinking we are like to stay here till Gabriel sounds the last trumpet, if Molang comes this way soon," Amos said to me in a whisper. "I do not count the French as enemies greatly to be feared while we fight in the woods; but he is worse than a fool who would belittle the danger in case any considerable body of Indians appear."

"And do you say that, Amos, meaning it is your idea the major is overbrave?"

"It would be no fault in him if he were that, and we know he is. I spoke only of what you well understand: that we are like to stay here long, if the red imps come in any number."

"Do you envy those who, being sick, returned to Fort Edward?" I asked, more in jest than in earnest, for I would not have allowed another to thus question Amos Cowden's courage.

"You know, Zenas, that he who desired to go back could have done so, and did I show any inclination to leave my comrades?"

"No, lad, I but jested. I would like to hear why you thought it necessary to state what all of us know full well."

"Perhaps it would hearten me a bit to put into words that which is in my mind."

"Are you suddenly grown timorous?" I asked, smiling, but not daring to laugh, lest I break the silence.

"I am, in good truth, Zenas Seabury; but at the same time I hold it is no shame. I am thinking that this, our first service for the King, is like to be our last."

"That I grant you, lad, and what more? We came of our own free will, and the major did but accept of our service, as we requested."

"Aye, Zenas, and being here, we shall do our best; yet now I have a favour to ask for the future. Do you remember the story Cyrus Litchfield told of his brother Robert's fate?"

"But why do you conjure up such pictures at this time, Amos?" I asked, almost petulantly.

"Because our ending is like to be that of his, unless we prepare against it in advance. You remember, Cyrus said Robert was tied with green withes to a tree; that the red fiends shot arrows into him, taking good care none inflicted a deadly wound, until he was fairly bristling with them, and then a slow fire was kindled under his feet, in such a manner that the wind had full sweep, thus ploughing the smoke away, which prevented him from being suffocated; that he was upwards of five hours dying."

There had come into my mind, before Amos spoke, this story which Cyrus Litchfield told, and Robert was scarce a year older than we; but I put it away hastily, lest it make me cowardly.

Now I was almost angered because my comrade had brought it so fresh to mind, and said, more hotly than I would have done had I stopped an instant to consider how near we both were to death:

"If you can bring before you, at such time, nothing better than this horrible picture, it were well you had gone with the sick, back to Fort Edward, for of a verity you will do no service here."

"Do not be angered, Zenas. I spoke with a purpose, but it was not to recall horrors simply for the sake of repeating them."

"To what end, then, have you spoken?"

"To ask this favour: if it should so be that we attack Molang's force, and are worsted, as it seems positive we must be, do you keep the last bullet for me. I will promise to do the same for you. Knowing that I have your word, I shall no longer fear Robert Litchfield's fate, and can fight with better heart to the last."

Now was the lad showing himself of braver metal than I, and, acting on the impulse of the moment, I flung both my arms around him.

He returned the embrace, and while one might have counted twenty, we two sat there, strengthened by thoughts of the friendship which each entertained for the other, as well as heartened by the promise of what should be done, when the last hour came.

Because of having made arrangements to avoid pain in the future, we were not minded to neglect precautions in the present, and set about strengthening that portion of the wall where we were stationed, working so long as the twilight permitted.

It was as if Israel Putnam never remained in a single spot two minutes at a time. Here and there, from one end of the fortification to the other, he walked cautiously, as though following the trail of the foe, seeing to it that every man of our little band was on the alert, and ever ready to speak such word as might hearten.

When it came so dark we could do no more than remain silent and motionless, trusting to our ears to give us warning of the approach of the foe, I insisted that Amos sleep while I watched, and thus, turn and turn about, should we two pass the night.

Not until I had promised to awaken him within an hour, did the dear lad consent to the plan, and thus we spent the time until daybreak, expecting each instant to be engaged in conflict, yet hearing nothing to betoken the presence of an enemy.

Why it was that all of us who watched behind the breastworks on the shore of South Bay should have been so positive the enemy would come this night, I know not; but be that as it may, we were happily disappointed when the sun rose again, and more than one ventured the opinion that Major Rogers's division, not ours, would be the first to discover the foe.

"We shall meet them here," Israel Putnam said, as though he could read the future. "We shall meet them here, lads of Connecticut, and however strong they may be in numbers, the meeting will be a sorry one for them."

CHAPTER II.

THE ATTACK.

OF what passed during the next eight and forty hours, there is little need I should speak, because it would simply be to use the same words over and over again.

We remained on the alert, as may well be imagined, Amos and I, side by side, and only once after that second night did he speak of the promise we had made each other.

Then it was, when our time of waiting had well-nigh come to an end, that he said, as if referring to what was already beyond a peradventure:

"We'll not forget what it may be necessary to do for each other before many hours, and our hearts will not fail us at the last moment?"

"I remember as if the promise were but just made," was my reply; and from that time the subject was not brought up again.

During this eight and forty hours we lived on short allowance, as can well be fancied, for the troops in those days did not carry large supplies of provisions with them, —each man run his own commissary department when we were on the march, save it might be immediately after having left the outposts of a settlement.

It was shortly after sunset, on the night of the fourth day after we made camp at the Elbow, when one of the men, whom I knew had been out on the scout, came into the fortification, if such a term could be given our rude approach at a defence, hurriedly, and with an expression on his face which told that he brought news of importance.

At the moment, Major Putnam stood near to where Amos and I had posted ourselves, and thus it was we heard the full report of the scout.

The man was an Indian who had taken service because of his friendliness for Israel Putnam, and that which he said I knew could be depended on beyond peradventure.

"Molang, with no less than four hundred Indians and a hundred Frenchmen, has made a portage from Lake George, landing near to Shelving Rock, and is now approaching," the scout said, speaking in his native tongue, which was not unfamiliar to either Amos or I, we having learned it from no less a person than this same redskin himself.

It is true he did not utter the very words I have repeated; but in his way that was what the information meant.

Although he reported the number of the enemy at five hundred, it appeared as if our major was fearful lest he should not have an opportunity of meeting them with his squad of thirty-five men, and he asked, with much of anxiety in his tones:

"Are you certain they come this way, Sewatis?"

"I remained near by until the foremost began launching their canoes. They will pass in half an hour."

"Faith, but you are giving to us little time for preparation; and yet I do not know that we need it," the major said, as if speaking to himself, and then, turning to me, he added:

"Did you understand what Sewatis said, Seabury?"

"Yes, sir; it was he who taught me how to speak his lingo."

"Then see to it you remain on the alert. Remember, not the slightest sound, no matter how fair a target may present itself, until I give the word."

Then he moved from one to the other of our little party, telling of the news which had been brought, and, as I suppose, giving some orders to each man in turn, until all of us who were then behind the wall of the rock knew what might be expected.

At this moment there were but three, now that Sewatis had returned, who were out on the scout,— Lieutenant Durkee and two men who lived nearabout Guilford.

"In half an hour there will be fifteen of the enemy against every one of us," Amos whispered, softly. "It is odds such as pleases the major, and yet I should be better content were we more nearly equal in force."

"These breastworks, and the fact that they will be in canoes when we fire upon them, give us big advantage, even though we be small in numbers," I replied, determined to keep in mind whatsoever might serve to hearten me, for of a verity I was growing weak-kneed at the thought of the desperate encounter in which we must soon take part.

At this moment, the major glided noiselessly as a panther past where we were lying, and seemingly as eager as such a brute when he is in search of prey.

We held our peace, lest he should reprove us for even so much as a whisper, which would surely be a grave offence when you remember the nature of those whom we knew were approaching.

It was as if nature would aid us in the coming struggle.

The night was so calm that the flame of a candle would hardly have flickered; not a cloud could be seen in the sky, and it was the time of the full moon.

Below us, the water, so narrow at this point that a musket-ball would readily carry to the opposite shore, and had a leaf floated by on the surface of the lake, it could easily have been distinguished from where we lay.

If the red murderers ventured around the Elbow, they must pass within fifty yards of our ambush, and even though we were worsted in the end, as I doubted not would be the case, certain it was we should make havoc among them before they were recovered from the first surprise.

I don't know how it may have been with Amos, but, as for me, every one of those twenty-five or thirty minutes which were spent there, expecting each instant to see the foremost of the fleet of canoes appear on the moonlit waters, was like unto ten ordinary minutes, and I thought again and again that even the conflict, unequal though it must be, would seem like a relief.

When the suspense was ended, it was suddenly, and though the coming of the enemy had been expected, I fancied more than one of our comrades started in surprise when the first craft appeared in view.

Involuntarily I glanced back towards where I had last seen the major.

He was standing with up-raised hand, as if to command silence, and, at the same instant, peering gravely out over the water, a look on his face which, to my mind, would have boded ill for Molang's murderous crew had we been in greater numbers.

Brief as was the time of my looking back, when I glanced towards the water again, it was as if the entire surface was covered with canoes filled with painted savages, and I wondered how Sewatis could have made such a mistake as to numbers, for it seemed that already I saw more than a thousand men, and as yet the entire French portion of the force had not appeared.

Amos was literally quivering with excitement, and I put out my hand to steady the flint-lock, which had nearly dropped from his grasp.

Had it been other than Amos Cowden who thus trembled, I would have said he was afraid; but I knew my comrade better than that, and had seen him when the Indians, while not as numerous, were where it was possible to do us more harm.

Instead of looking at the foremost boats, I kept my

eyes fixed upon the point from where they appeared, that I might see the last; and yet the end came not when it was as if a quarter of an hour had passed, while, all in

front of me, the moonlit water was darkened by this murderous crew.

Once more I glanced towards the major, saying to myself that surely now was come the time when he would give the signal.

His hand was still raised as if to command silence, and I wondered why we were held back when not a man among us could fail of hitting his target.

Already were the foremost of the canoes past our breastworks, and then suddenly came a noise so slight that, under other circumstances, I would have hardly given it heed; but now it was as a clap of thunder in my ears.

One of the Guilford men had, perhaps, while shaking with the same ague fit that affected Amos, struck his musket against a rock.

As if it had been the report of a gun, those in the foremost canoes ceased paddling, and gazed around suspiciously.

So clear was the night that I could even see the weapons in their hands as the painted imps prepared for the attack.

Some of the paddlers, not knowing whence the sound proceeded, and fearing to venture on, sent the ashen blades deep in the water, as they forced their light craft backward, with the result that before one could have counted thirty, the whole fleet was jammed together, the current setting them directly towards our ambush.

I was certain now had come the time when the word to fire would be given, and yet the major remained silent.

We could hear the enemy below talking rapidly in low tones, as if discussing the cause of the alarm, and then, some decision having been arrived at, the canoes were put about,—the foe so valiant when unprotected women and children stood before them, were about to retreat because of a noise which might have been a chipmunk!

It was while all this light craft lay in a mass, the canoes coming closely together because of the attempt to turn them, that Israel Putnam said, in a low, sharp tone:

"Now, boys! Don't waste a bullet!"

I question if, in that first volley, when no more than thirty-five balls were sent towards the water, as small a number of wounds were inflicted; some of the bullets must have done double work, and I believe, in fact, I am positive in my own mind, that more than fifty of the enemy were disabled.

There was no need for the major to give an order to reload.

Every one of us knew that his life depended upon the quickness of his movements then.

Now was our advantage, and if we failed to take it, then indeed were we undone.

I know not how it might have been with the others, but as for me, I was already ramming the balls into the barrel of my musket when Molang's crew got their wits together sufficiently to fire in our direction, and then I heard Amos laugh, for the discharge was as harmless as if the weapons had been pointed towards the sky.

Again we sent a shower of lead, not this time as one man, but in a scattering volley, each discharging his weapon as soon as it was loaded, and again do I believe that more than one bullet did double work.

It seemed as if in every canoe were two or three disabled savages; yet the fire was returned, and four times was this repeated before I heard a cry from our men.

Then it was him from Guilford who had unwittingly given the alarm, and an instant later Sewatis, who had been standing near to Major Putnam, suddenly dropped his flint-lock.

Twice more, six volleys in all, did Molang's crew fire at us, and then I believe that fiend in human shape began to understand how few we were in numbers, for such fact could readily be seen when the muskets were discharged at intervals.

We heard a loud word of command from him, when suddenly ten or twelve canoes were detached from the mass that was being sent in hot haste up South Bay, and, skirting as near as might be to the opposite shore, were making as if to attack us from the rear.

It was Israel Putman who commanded our forces, which is as if I said it was a man ready for any emergency, and watchful ever for the slightest movement on the part of the foe.

Hardly had these twelve canoes started past the Elbow, when he ordered Lieutenant Durkee to take twelve men and see to it they did not land.

We had little time to spend on this party who were gone to protect our rear. The force was thus weakened by thirteen men; two others were wounded, and there were but twenty able bodies among us.

Even though we had done our best before, we must make yet greater exertions.

We, meaning Amos and I, had discharged our muskets until powder-horns and bullet-pouches were well-nigh emptied, and then the last of the canoes had disappeared around the point.

It was time to get some ammunition, and I went from man to man, asking who could give me of their store, until I had come to the last, and learned what caused me to grow even more timorous than when I first knew our little band of thirty-five was to attack five hundred of Molang's scoundrelly savages, — our powder and ball were well-nigh exhausted!

"You must do the best you can with what is left, lad," Major Putnam said, hearing me tell Amos the result of the mission. "Make every bullet count, and then, if God wills, we'll stand back to back until succour comes or we fall."

It was a brave speech; but at the moment I would rather have had powder and ball than all his heartening words, for there was behind them a suggestion not at all to my liking.

"Remember that we are to keep one bullet each for the other," Amos whispered to me, in a tone so low that the major could not have overheard him had he made the attempt.

Then, leaning over the wall of rock, pushing away here and there one of the trees which had marked our fortification, that we might the better keep watch on that stretch of water directly opposite the point, we waited, fully believing Molang would return once more, when his scoundrelly crew were recovered somewhat from the drubbing they had received.

Then it was from the rear we heard the sound of firing, and knew Lieutenant Durkee, with his little squad, was doing what he might to prevent the painted foe from landing.

When, after perhaps five minutes, the rattle of musketry died away, we asked ourselves, hardly daring to ask each other, if he had succeeded in his work, been cut down, or was run short of ammunition.

Half an hour later we knew the former of the three possibilities was the fact, for then the canoes which had lately gone down the bay were seen creeping up near the opposite shore to rejoin the main fleet, and they were hardly past our fortification when the lieutenant returned.

He had repulsed the foe without having lost a man.

He reported that his task had been an easy one; the savages, cowardly save when all the odds are in their favour, had speedily beat a retreat when he made the first opposition to their landing, and that which he had done was as if he had been driving a flock of sheep.

As before the coming of Molang's horde, everywhere was silence.

Again it seemed as if we were alone on the shore of the bay, with no human beings near, and yet we knew that less than a mile distant were those who thirsted for our blood, and would strain every nerve and muscle to kill us.

Now were the scouts sent out once more, and we who were unharmed resumed our task of watching when nothing was to be seen.

THE ATTACK. 45

Israel Putnam began his stealthy pacing to and fro, stopping only when he halted beside the wounded men to make certain they were not suffering for lack of anything which we might give, and from time to time sending forth one on the scout.

"Why might we not do our share of that work?" Amos asked, suddenly, of me. "Surely we are able, having done it often before, and I warrant you, Zenas, we could perform our part without being ashamed before some of those men whom I have seen at work."

"We may not do it because the major has bidden others," I replied.

"Yet if we ask as a favour, he might permit us."

"But that I would not do. Israel Putnam knows whether we are to be trusted or not, and if he fails to summon us, it is not our place to remind him, lest peradventure he may say we are of value only in our own estimation."

"Almost anything would be better than lying here, knowing that Molang's crew may be creeping up on us each instant."

"They would creep the same were we scouting."

"Aye; but it is less painful to know a thing, than to imagine it," Amos replied, with a laugh which had in it very little of mirth, and then he fell silent.

I think it was near to morning when all those who had been sent out to spy upon the enemy came back at the same time, and we could have guessed the news they brought before the foremost reported to the major:

"Both the Indians and Frenchmen have landed and are marching this way, coming in such order as to surround our force."

For the moment Israel Putnam appeared to me as if he was minded to give them battle regardless of the disparity in numbers, but then there must have come into his mind — for he was not a careless man — the thought of how soon a battle would be finished should we begin one, owing to our lack of ammunition, and, in an instant, as it were, his plan had been formed.

Detailing two men to accompany the wounded, he ordered them to proceed by the nearest course to the fort.

"As for ourselves, sir?" the lieutenant stopped to ask.

"There is but one course left us, and that is to beat a retreat."

It was done as quietly and leisurely as if there was no reason why we should hasten.

The men were bidden to gather up their belongings, and to follow the lieutenant silently, in single file.

As for Israel Putnam, he remained in the rear, and I doubt not but that it would have pleased him had the enemy come so near as to give good excuse for a brush.

Amos and I were about midway in the line. Because of lacking years, I suppose it was fancied we might also lack courage, and it hurt me that we were not given a better chance to show Israel Putnam we were more to be depended upon than those men from Guilford, who were well in the advance.

We marched silently and rapidly for upwards of an hour, going not towards the fort, but rather in the direction of Deer Pasture Mountain, to avoid the enemy.

It seemed positive we must have given him the slip, when suddenly, from out among the foliage, while yet no person could be seen, came a volley of musketry, and one of our small band fell.

CHAPTER III.

DESERTING THE WOUNDED.

WHEN the shower of lead came out from amid the foliage without warning, we naturally supposed some portion of Molang's forces had succeeded in swinging around to cut off our retreat, and the echoes had hardly died away when Amos whispered, hoarsely:

"Remember to save the last bullet!"

In view of the fact that our ammunition was so well nigh spent we could not afford to throw away a single shot, instead of replying to this musket-fire as would ordinarily have been done, Israel Putnam gave the order to "Charge."

We had been marching in single file, but when the first interruption came our small band clustered together until, by the time the major had spoken, we were a compact body; and although it was no pleasant thing to make a charge amid the foliage, upon, as we supposed, a company who would skulk from tree to tree, there was no hesitation in obeying the order.

Before we were well in motion, however, a voice, coming from that point whence the firearms had been discharged, cried:

"Hold! We are friends!"

Involuntarily we halted the merest fraction of time, and then came most likely to all, as it did to Amos and I, the thought that this was but a trick to prevent action on our part until another volley could be thrown among us; and we were moving forward without awaiting a second word of command, when Israel Putnam halted the force, as he shouted to the unseen detachment who had treated us as foes:

"If we be friends, as you say, why that volley?"

"We are from Fort Edward," the voice replied, and, almost at the same instant, a British officer stepped into view. "The scouts brought in word of how hotly you were pressed, and we are sent to cover your retreat."

There was not a man among us who could well control his temper at this moment. We provincials had little faith in the abilities of the trained British soldiers in such warfare as must be waged when savages were our foes, and this blunder, which might have cost a dozen lives, was inexcusable.

Even Israel Putnam lost control of his temper, and cried, hotly, while the red-coated officer was advancing:

"Whether you be friends or foes, you deserve death for doing so slight execution with as fair a shot. Had we been of the French, with the ordinary backing of savages, that volley must have been your last."

The King's troops had as little confidence in us provincials as we in them, and this officer's face flushed at being thus reproved, — not for the blunder, but because, while firing from ambush, he had succeeded in wounding only one man.

He came towards the major with the air of one who has a grievance, and during ten minutes or more the two held converse.

We of the rank and file could only guess at what passed between our major and the King's officer, but in our minds we knew who was the better soldier, so far as this kind of warfare went, and I felt much as did Amos, when he whispered to me:

"I only hope that red-coated gentleman will hear all which I believe is in Israel Putnam's mind to say."

While these two were talking, the older provincials dressed the wound of him who had been stricken down, which fortunately was a slight one, and Amos and I were watching the operation when our major called, sharply:

"Zenas Seabury!"

I started as if this summons was a reproof, and then, immediately after, realising that I had committed no fault, stepped forward, Amos following, although his name had not been called.

The older members of our division looked jealously upon us when the major, having parted company with the British officer, stepped back several paces, lest any of our people should hear what was said.

"Although you two be but lads, I know the stock from whence you sprung, and can trust you better than some of those who claim to have had more experience. The detachment will, of course, move towards Fort Edward, with the idea that, before arriving there, we shall be joined by the other two divisions. It is my purpose to send out as many as can be safely spared, to make known to Major Rogers and Captain Dalyell the reason for our retreat, lest they be cut off. Are you two lads of the mind to venture on the work?"

"Aye, sir, that we are," I answered, promptly, for the service suited me far better than this playing at the soldier when we had little or no idea of military duty; and Amos stepped more closely to my side, in order that the reply might be taken as his.

"Heed well the dangers which must be encountered; remember that we are most likely surrounded by French and Indians to the number of perhaps a thousand or more; that in event of failure a cruel death must follow."

This Israel Putnam said almost as if he would dissuade us from accepting the service he himself had proposed.

"We know all that full well, sir," I replied, taking Amos by the hand, that it should appear as if both had spoken. "You are kind enough to say you know the stock from which we have sprung. You also know, sir, what we can do, for this is not the first time we have been in your company, although never before as a King's soldier."

"Aye, lad; save for that I had not proposed the enterprise."

"Then you can understand, sir," I continued, emboldened by his kindly manner, "that we would willingly face any danger rather than refuse whatsoever you might propose."

"I believe you, lad, and it is because of that, that I point out all the dangers, preferring rather that you should go of your own free will than because I sent you."

"And in good truth, sir, such service is more to our liking than remaining with the company, when we can do no better than the veriest coward among them, and even that is denied while the ammunition runs so low," Amos replied.

"It is well said, lad, and we will let that end the matter. I can give you no instructions other than to find Rogers and Dalyell as soon as may be. Tell them we are making our way as slowly as is consistent with safety towards Fort Edward, and, if possible, will camp near Fort Anne, on Clear River, where I hope they may come up with us. You shall be plentifully supplied with ammunition, because it is no crime to lighten the pouches of the redcoats, who should have used their charges with better results when they fired upon us by mistake. Consult your best judgment as to how the mission may be accomplished. It was Rogers's intention to have halted within ten or twelve miles from where we made our stand, and Dalyell must be nearabout that vicinity."

He had scarce ceased speaking, when two red-coated soldiers advanced, having been sent most likely by their officer, to fill our powder-horns and shot-pouches to overflowing.

A third came forward with such store of dried venison

and corn meal as could be spared, and we were ready for the enterprise.

Amos would have set out immediately; but I held him in check a moment, that we might learn if the major had any further commands for us.

It was as if we no longer had an existence so far as Israel Putnam was concerned.

He was talking with two of the older provincials, most likely sending them out on the same mission with which we were entrusted, and I hesitated no longer.

"You are right, Amos. We will go at once," and, without a thought of leave-taking, we struck off into the wilderness in the direction from which the squad had just come.

If Amos Cowden and I had had no previous experience in such work, I doubt not but that we would soon have been gobbled up by Molang's painted imps, for they were everywhere around us, as we learned before having left the detachment a mile in the rear.

These murdering villains were as thick as blackberries in September, and one had need to take heed to his every step lest suddenly he come full upon one.

No less than eight did we see while we traversed barely more than a mile in distance, and I thought — for Amos and I dared not speak one to the other even in a whisper, — that perchance we were in no greater danger than the detachment, for it seemed to me they were already completely surrounded.

After a distance of two miles more had been covered, it was as if we had passed the danger-line, and were beyond the painted scouts, for now we neither heard their movements nor saw a fresh trail, and by this time it was nigh to noon, although we had started early in the morning.

When one considers well all that may be around him before he dares advance a single step, the progress is exceedingly slow, and we were minded to use the excess of precaution rather than not enough.

It seemed to me that we would be safe in halting sufficiently long to eat a leisurely meal, for since the night previous we had partaken of food only in fragments, now and then a mouthful.

We were tired, rather because of anxiety than on account of actual labour performed, and ate slowly, that we might enjoy our halt ; but it was as if we had no more than begun before certain sounds proclaimed the approach of man or beast.

It can well be imagined that we took our precautions as if positive the noises were caused by the former, and, after hurriedly obliterating all signs of having halted in that place, we crouched behind the trees, for whoever approached was coming directly towards us, with such lack of prudence as caused me to believe they were neither Indians nor of our party.

Then, when perhaps five minutes had passed, to my surprise we saw advancing those two of Israel Putnam's command who had been detailed to accompany the wounded to Fort Edward.

We stepped into full view, and there was an incautious exclamation of satisfaction from the men as they saw us.

"Have you taken leave of your wits that you speak so loudly here, when we know, beyond a peradventure, the woods are filled with Molang's crew?" Amos asked, in an angry whisper, although these newcomers were older than we by many years.

"You are frightened without cause, lad," one of them replied. "Molang's forces are making straight for the fort."

"Then they have left a good many behind, for we have seen not less than twenty scouts since leaving Major Putnam's command; but how is it you are here? Where are the wounded men?"

In an instant the expression on the faces of these two changed, and I knew without being told that some disaster had overtaken them.

"We were pursued by the savages before having gone two miles," one of them said, "and to escape was impossible, while we remained with the wounded."

"But surely you did not desert them?" I cried; and these cowards must have understood what was in my mind, for they said, like men who excuse themselves to lawful accusers:

"It would have been death for all four had we remained, and the wounded themselves proposed that we leave them. Better two escape than that four be killed."

"I would not say that, had I been one of the four," Amos muttered, speaking so low that I question whether his words were overheard save by me.

"When the pursuit became so hot that we knew it was

impossible to escape, Sewatis insisted we should leave them to their fate," one of the men said, speaking hurriedly, as if he would tell all his story before it was possible for us to check him. "Had there been any chances we could have saved their lives, this thing would not have happened; but, as it was, death staring four in the face if we remained, and the chance that two might escape if we fled, we followed the Indian's advice. So close were Molang's crew, that ere we were out of sight two brutes came up, and before he was tomahawked I saw our comrade fire three shots, each of which marked the death of one of the foe. By that time we had succeeded in putting a greater distance between us and the enemy, and saw nothing more; but it seemed certain Sewatis was reserved as prisoner, because no further shots were fired while we were in that vicinity. Which way are you two going?"

"Down the shore, to open communication with Major Rogers," I replied, curtly, not caring to hold further converse with these men who would abandon helpless comrades without making one effort towards saving their lives.

"And Major Putnam's force?"

"Is surrounded by a thousand or more French and Indians, and trying to gain Fort Edward."

"Then it would seem as if there was little hope we could rejoin them?" the man who told the story of the desertion asked.

I nodded my head, but made no reply.

"It will, perhaps, be better that we remain with you;" and one would have said from the manner in which the

DESERTING THE WOUNDED. 61

man spoke that he believed we should be pleased with such comrades.

I glanced towards Amos and fancied I read from the expression on his face thoughts similar to mine, therefore said, without compunction, even though these cowards were our elders:

"We shall be better content alone, and the danger is far too great for you to take part in."

The man appeared as if astonished because we did not welcome his company, and made reply:

"If the woods are so full of Indians as you think, surely there is greater safety in numbers."

It angered me that he should not understand when I had already spoken so plainly, and, without further care as to whether his feelings were hurt, I said, sharply:

"When the numbers are increased by those who desert wounded comrades, Amos Cowden and I would rather travel alone."

This time the fellow got through his thick head somewhat of my meaning, and for a moment I fancied he was on the point of giving way to anger, which would have troubled me but little; but he checked himself, and turned aside to speak with his companion, whereupon I motioned to Amos, and, before the two comrades were well aware of our movements, we had slipped off among the foliage.

"Better take no rest at all, than have as companions such as they," Amos whispered, in a tone of disgust, and we finished our meal while travelling.

We were making as nearly as we could, not being thoroughly familiar with the country, a straight course for Black Mountain, counting on continuing along its base, beyond Sugar Loaf, to that portion of Lake Champlain opposite Bluff Point, on the shores of Lake George, where was a portage; and it was reasonable

to suppose Major Rogers would have to halt there, knowing Molang's crew might cross at that point.

It seemed now as if we might travel more rapidly, for, after having left the cowards two miles behind, there were no signs of the enemy, and it appeared certain all had come over from Lake George by the Shelving Rock Portage.

Now we pushed on at our best pace, spending but little time in reconnoitring the ground, and before nightfall had accomplished the mission.

Major Rogers's force was camped in the locality we had decided they would select, and his scouts were making a circle roundabout the place, fully four miles from the main body.

In this case, the major was neglecting no precautions, and it would have been better had he continued to act with as much prudence.

As a matter of course, we were given a friendly reception, and, after having delivered our message, were told that Captain Dalyell was yet three miles further on.

"I will send some one else to warn him. You have travelled far enough to make up this day's work," he said, kindly; and both Amos and I were willing to rest, for there was no honour to be gained in pushing ahead to the captain, since all danger was now apparently passed. I had feared Major Rogers might hesitate to turn back in response to Israel Putnam's request; but he was not such a fool, and word was given that the command would set out as soon after daybreak as Captain Dalyell's force arrived.

Having been served with a bountiful supply of deer meat, we two laid ourselves down to make up for the sleep we had lost on the night previous, and there was no thought in my mind but that we would rejoin Israel Putnam, in company with this force, until Amos whispered, just as my eyes were closing in slumber:

"Is it your purpose to stay here until this detachment sets out?"

"Why should we not?" I asked, in surprise.

"Then you count on marching with them?"

"It will be safer."

"Of that I am not so certain. There are too many red uniforms here to please me, and surely you and I have seen enough of the King's disciplined soldiers to understand that they are not pleasant companions at such a time. I have no desire to lose my hair because of their blundering through the forest with a noise sufficient to give the alarm a mile away."

"What do you propose?" I asked, not pleased with the idea of parting company with this force, even though there were redcoats among them.

"That we gain what sleep we can 'twixt now and midnight, and then set out by ourselves."

"Such a course may not be to Major Rogers's liking."

"Where will be the harm if he fails to approve of it? We are under Israel Putnam's command, and have no orders from him to stay with this force. Our mission has been accomplished. It now remains for us to return to our proper command."

"If your mind is set on such a course, I will do as you propose, although it does not seem wise."

"Show me how much wisdom there is in loitering, and my mouth is closed."

This I could not do, for I knew full well what a dangerous companion a redcoat was in the forest, and, failing in any reasonable argument, I allowed the matter to remain as my comrade had proposed.

We would set out at midnight, and join the Connecticut men under Israel Putnam.

CHAPTER IV.

SEWATIS.

THE men of Rogers's command, with whom we talked before laying down for a nap, did not appear to think the danger which threatened the English forces, in this vicinity, to be very great.

It was all in vain that Amos and I repeated what the scouts had reported regarding the strength of the French and their Indian allies, for each man would hark back to the statement we had made concerning our attack upon the greater portion of Molang's crew.

It was as if they set us down as liars on one point or the other.

If Major Putnam had really attacked and driven off Molang and his painted hordes with but thirty-five men, and only a small supply of ammunition, then there were nowhere near as many savages as we had stated.

In case it was to be allowed that the reports brought in by our scouts were correct, then had we spoken falsely in telling of the attack.

I tired of trying to make the thick-headed ones believe that both stories were absolutely true, and gave up the task after ten minutes, while Amos held his peace, as if in a fit of the sulks, from the first moment one of his statements was discredited.

Do not understand me as saying that Major Rogers looked upon our report as being false; he apparently accepted every word in good truth, but I am of the opinion he privately believed we had stretched the story considerably in order to make ourselves appear in the light of heroes.

All this I repeat here lest it be supposed Amos and I proposed to return to Israel Putnam's command alone, simply because of the English soldiers under Major Rogers.

It is true this was one strong reason, not because we would belittle his Majesty's forces as soldiers, but owing to the fact that they did not understand Indian tactics, and, consequently, were dangerous companions in the forest.

However, as has been said, we decided to return alone, and to such end asked the corporal of the guard to see that we were turned out shortly before midnight.

It lacked nearly an hour of that time when he shook us roughly, as was necessary because of the heaviness of our slumbers, and we arose slowly, I for one regretting that we had decided to push on alone, since we were thus deprived of so much sleep as seemed necessary.

Once being fully awake, however, there was no thought in our minds of lying down again, and, after begging such a quantity of smoked venison as would suffice to provide us with food during the next four and twenty hours, we set out on the return.

Major Rogers had made no objection to our departure; and I fancied, because of our willingness to undertake the journey alone when we might have ample escort, he was more than ever inclined to doubt certain portions of our report.

It was almost as light as at noonday, save where the shadows were most dense, and with the big, round moon as a guide he would be worse than a fool who could go astray.

It was not likely Molang's crew had come this way, even though that crafty leader had fullest information regarding these two divisions which lay between him and Israel Putnam's men. He would remain where he was, or press on towards the fort, content to wait until Major Rogers's force came to him, as they must finally do.

Therefore, as Amos and I reckoned, a full two-thirds of the distance could be traversed without much fear of being molested, and, once well clear of the encampment, we pressed forward rapidly, arriving at what we believed to be dangerous ground shortly before sunrise.

Then, the moon having set, it was so dark that I insisted on remaining where we were until the day broke, rather than take the chances of coming suddenly upon a band of savages, and two hours later we were not sorry for having done so.

It can well be supposed that we had no inclination to indulge in more slumber, but we disposed of ourselves in whatsoever manner was most comfortable, with all due regard to safety, and breakfasted bountifully on such fare as we had procured before leaving Major Rogers's encampment.

Before the new day had fully come, we could see close around us such signs as told that we must be in the very midst of Molang's friends.

The trail was fresh on every hand, as we peered anxiously out from our hiding-place in the thicket, and, even as we gazed, the odour of smoke came strong to our nostrils.

There was no need for me to give words to what was in my mind.

I glanced towards Amos, and could read from his face that he understood how narrowly we had escaped walking directly upon enemies who found greater pleasure in the capture of one man than the killing of three, because in the former case they could satisfy their love of inflicting torture upon the helpless.

Even though we were in such a dangerous locality, it was absolutely necessary we incur yet greater peril, for our very lives depended upon knowing whether we were near to the main body of savages, or only a party of scouts. And this information must be gained at once, before the painted friends were fully astir for mischief.

It is best not to spend too much time thinking of such a task, lest one grow timorous, therefore I started at once, wriggling my way through the underbrush even as our enemies would have done, and, as I flatter myself, moving with as little noise as any of Molang's evil ones.

In less than twenty minutes, even at our slow method

of advance, we had arrived where we could have a full view of the savages, so near had we unwittingly come to them in the darkness, and with the first glimpse I was like to have cried out in sorrowful surprise.

Tied by green withes to a tree, in such position that he could move neither hand nor foot, was Sewatis, the friendly Indian, whom those cowardly curs we met had deserted while wounded, to face, with his brave companion, their bloodthirsty pursuers.

The white man had sold his life at a good price, as the cowards told us, having killed three of the redskins before they buried a hatchet in his brain, and Sewatis, he who had ever been a friend to Amos and I, was to taste of the torture.

That his suffering would come soon I had little doubt, for these fiends could not burden themselves with a prisoner long; and instantly the thought flashed into my mind that it was our solemn duty to give him aid.

While helpless, he had been deserted by white men, and now white boys should show him they were not of such cowardly kidney.

Again I looked at Amos, and again he nodded his head.

Even though we were willing, I failed to understand how we might give the poor fellow aid.

There were eight savages in the party, six of whom appeared to be yet asleep, while the two who had built the fire were moving to and fro in such a manner that we could not so much as have advanced a dozen paces towards them without being discovered.

It was plain that nothing could be done at once, and yet we might expect that the number of the enemy would be added to rather than diminished as time wore on.

Amos touched me on the shoulder, and, as I looked around, pointed to his powder-horn and then his musket, as if to say we might succeed by making a sudden attack.

I shook my head decidedly, for such a wild plan was not to be thought of, unless we were disposed to sacrifice our own lives with but little hope of being able to accomplish the purpose.

As well as could be done by gestures, I gave him to understand we must wait, in the hope matters might take a turn in our favour, and it was plain to be seen that he had little faith in delay.

I knew full well, however, that, if we should empty our muskets with deadly aim, we would have six savages upon us before we could reload, and no one might say how many more were within ear-shot.

It was heart-breaking work, crouching there in the underbrush, not daring so much as to draw a long breath, for already was the torture beginning for Sewatis.

Neither of the two Indians passed without dealing a blow, or otherwise ill-treating him, and when the whole crew were awake the party set about hurling their knives and tomahawks at the helpless prisoner, taking good care, meanwhile, not to inflict a deadly blow.

Sewatis was bleeding from a dozen slight wounds before the fiends devoured the morning meal, and both Amos and I could see that he had nerved himself for the worst.

It was positive he would not give the murdering scoundrels the satisfaction of hearing from his lips so much as a moan of pain.

As I watched this man facing the most horrible of deaths, the thought came into my mind that we might give him some slight relief of mind by announcing our presence, and even at the moment an opportunity presented itself.

He was staring vacantly in our direction; the savages were intent upon the half-cooked meat they were pulling from off the embers, and not a single one facing us.

At risk of discovery I parted the foliage from in front of me, and waved my hand.

Instantly the look of vacancy fled from his eyes, and in its place came one of relief and hope.

Even though we failed in our purpose, we had shown our willingness to aid, and, after the treatment he had received from those who deserted him and his comrade, this must have been gratifying to the poor fellow.

Now, watching him closely, I understood he was revolving some plan in his mind, and from that instant kept my eyes fixed upon him, ready for the first showing he should make of his thoughts.

When perhaps five minutes had passed, he looked meaningly towards the spot where we were concealed, and then began taunting his captors with cowardice in trying to starve him into displaying some sign of weakness.

Neither Amos nor I could understand all he said, for

he spoke in a language which differed somewhat from his own, but we could gather here and there enough to give us the meaning.

He told them what we all knew, that Molang himself fed his prisoners generously before torturing them to death, because it afforded him no pleasure in seeing a weak man give way suddenly, thus depriving him of perhaps several hours' pleasure; that a strong captive suffered more under the torture, and he had partaken of no food for twenty-four hours.

In short, he made out the case as if his own desire was to please them, declaring that he preferred to go fasting to death, since relief would thus come the sooner; but it sorrowed him to be in the power of such cowards that eight were afraid of one.

I failed to understand what he was aiming at, but soon saw that his taunts were having the desired effect.

Before the savages had satisfied their own hunger a short consultation was held among them, with the result that Sewatis was set free from the bonds, but closely guarded, lest he should make a sudden dash for liberty.

The wily prisoner affected to be exceedingly weak; it was as if he could not put one foot before another, and had not two of Molang's followers supported him I believe of a verity he would have fallen to the ground, in order the better to carry out his plan.

He was given a place near the fire, closely surrounded, however, and allowed to take from the embers several slices of meat, which he devoured as if famishing.

There was no question but that all this was being done in furtherance of some plan he had formed, and I ventured to whisper to Amos that we must be on the alert for any sudden move Sewatis might make.

It was well I warned my comrade, otherwise we might have been caught napping at the very instant quick action was necessary on our part.

Sewatis ate in a ravenous manner for five minutes or more, when suddenly he grasped the musket of the Indian seated nearest to him, leaped to his feet, and brought down the clubbed weapon on the head of its owner.

One could hardly have counted three from the instant he made the first movement until the savage lay dead; but short though the time was, we acted, because of being on the alert for something of the kind.

My musket was already levelled, the barrel resting over a stout twig, with the bead drawn on the beast to the right of Sewatis, and I fired, the report of my weapon mingling with that of Amos's.

It was only the merest fraction of time before Sewatis discharged the gun he held full at the breast of the savage in front of him, and in a twinkling, as you might say, four of the enemy were out of the fight.

Without being well aware of my movements, I sprang to my feet, and dashed forward, yelling at the full strength of my lungs, while Amos followed my example.

The Indians must have believed there was a large force behind us, otherwise we would not have dared to charge thus upon them, and, without waiting to strike a single blow, they fled in hot haste,—all save one, who was felled to the ground by Sewatis, even before he could turn to flee.

It was the most complete victory I ever saw, and could not have been effected had either Amos or I hesitated a single second after the red man gave the signal.

I sprang forward to grasp Sewatis's hand; but he knew

too well the value of time at this instant.

"Twenty more will soon be on us!" he cried, in his own language, as he stooped to supply himself with powder and ball from the bodies of the lifeless ones, who a few seconds previous were determined he should die the most painful death. "We have yet to save our lives, for the alarm has been given."

I waited for him to lead the way, knowing full well he alone among us three knew best what should be done, and before I could have counted five he started off at right angles with the course Major Rogers's men must follow in order to reach Fort Anne.

Hurriedly, as we ran, I told him that the troops were coming up the lake; but he did not change the course.

How long this flight continued I cannot say; I was so excited by our success as to have no idea of the passage of time; but this I am certain of, both Amos and I were well-nigh spent when the Indian finally slackened his speed.

He allowed us perhaps three minutes in which to regain our breath, and in that short interval we were able to explain from what quarter the second and third divisions might be expected.

"Molang knows all that; his scouts brought him word before midnight. We must make our way alone if we would live."

"We will follow wherever you lead," Amos replied, bravely, and I would have liked the speech much better had he added the words, "so long as we are able," for I mistrusted my ability to keep pace with the Indian if the flight was long continued.

During the next hour we doubled first this way and then that, until we were brought to a standstill by the sound of voices directly in our path, and we halted in astonishment that any man was venturesome enough to give his tongue free rein in such a place.

Shortly afterwards we came to understand that we were near to stumbling over a body of French troops, who were no better soldiers in the woods than the King's forces, and then Sewatis turned back, as if to retrace his steps.

It would be repeating almost the same words over and

over again if I should try to describe all we did on this day.

We were the hares, and Molang's crew the dogs who coursed us first this way and then that, coming within an ace of catching us a dozen times, but always baffled by the cunning of Sewatis.

Before we were with Israel Putnam's force again I reckoned that the Indian had saved our lives over and over; therefore were we quits, for it does not seem possible we could, unaided, have made our way through that forest, where it was as if every tree hid a foe, without being captured.

As it turned, however, we gained Major Putnam's encampment two hours after sunset, and were able to make a better report than any scout he had sent out, because of the fact that it was as if we had travelled over every yard of the land within a circle of ten miles.

The major was surprised at seeing Sewatis, as well he might be, for the cowards had returned to camp with their shameful story; and the Indian explained how he had been rescued, giving us so much praise a listener must have believed we deserved all the credit, when in fact it was Sewatis who had really rescued himself.

Both Amos and I tried to explain how small a part we played in the business, but even the major refused to listen, saying that it was enough to know we had risked our lives to aid a comrade, even though that comrade was an Indian.

"The cowards came in with their report, as if expecting

to be received in friendly fashion, after thus playing the cur," Israel Putnam said to us. "I could have killed them, and believed I was doing the province a good deed in taking off such vermin; but it would hardly have been the act of a soldier, therefore I simply turned them out of the camp, and every man of the force upheld me in so doing."

"Surely they cannot escape capture, surrounded as you are by Molang's savages!" Amos exclaimed.

"It will be only right if they are taken. Now tell me, what chance has Rogers and Dalyell of joining me?"

"It is only by coming up on the other side of Wood Creek that they can hope to do so," Sewatis replied, promptly, which proved that, while Amos and I were confused by the many turns and twists in our journey of the day, the Indian had gotten a good idea of how Molang's forces were distributed.

"Will you turn back, and warn them of what should be done?"

Believing this question was addressed to us, as well as the Indian, Amos and I both answered, "Yes;" but Israel Putnam brushed us aside as if we were untried lads.

"One can do the work better than three, and Sewatis is the man to go, providing he is willing to make the venture."

Instead of replying, the Indian walked rapidly away, bearing on his arm the musket taken from the Indian who would have tortured him to death, and I was disgruntled because of thus being overlooked.

"I can ill afford to spare one from this force," the major said, with his rare smile, "therefore you two must remain. There is more danger here than on the trail, of that you may be certain."

Then he turned from us, and after this last remark we were well content to remain.

CHAPTER V.

NEAR FORT ANNE.

I HAVE said that Israel Putnam's force was encamped on the border of Clear River, which is a fork of Wood Creek, before it joins East Creek, and less than a mile from Fort Anne.

Although Amos and I had found the woods roundabout so full of Indians, the major's scouts reported, as we learned shortly after Sewatis left camp, that Molang's crew were not advancing towards us, but rather contenting themselves with scouring the thicket to the eastward of Wood Creek, and holding that territory between us and Deer Mountain Pasture.

He is foolish, who, because his enemy is a brute, belittles the latter's ability.

That Molang hardly deserved the name of man is true; yet, at the same time, it must be confessed he was a crafty savage, and so well versed in his particular method of warfare as to be a dangerous foe. To suppose that he was not well aware of Israel Putnam's encampment, would be the same as saying that he was unusually thick-headed, when the reverse was the truth.

In discussing the matter among ourselves, Amos and I, we decided that Molang hesitated to attack us, lest he should frighten away the two divisions whose arrival we were expecting.

His force, counting three Frenchmen to be equal to one Indian, was so large that there could be little question as to the result if he attacked us, even after we were joined by Major Rogers's and Captain Dalyell's divisions.

We had come to spy out the enemy, and had found him in greater force than was at all pleasant.

Now, although we two said to ourselves that, should a regular battle ensue, the King's forces must be worsted, there was but little fear in our minds regarding the general outcome, so great was our faith in Israel Putnam's ability to extricate us from the difficulties; and the greatest care we had at that time was lest Major Rogers's division would be forced to go to their relief, and thus compass our own undoing.

There was ample time for Amos and I to discuss all these matters, because we were, as you might say, alone in the company, not being overly well acquainted with any of our companions-in-arms.

True it is, there were some Pomfret men among the party, with whom we passed the time of day when meeting, and we could call by name several of those from Guilford; but were not on such terms of acquaintance as would warrant our terming them comrades, or even friends.

Perhaps it was because Israel Putnam thought we had

done our share of extra duty, that he refrained from calling on us for any especial service during this time, when we lay waiting the coming of the divisions. We certainly could not feel jealous, since he had already sent us on a mission of no little danger, and in addition to accomplishing it we had saved Sewatis's life; therefore neither Amos nor I were fretting on account of thus remaining idle.

Yet it must not be supposed we were perfectly easy in our mind, for we had seen sufficient to tell us how numerous was Molang's crew, and knew beyond a peradventure that before many hours had passed we must be defending ourselves against overwhelming numbers.

It was because of this uneasiness that we had no desire for slumber, and were yet awake when, shortly before midnight, much to our surprise, Sewatis returned.

After making his report to the major, he sought us out, and thus we learned nearly as soon as did Israel Putnam of the condition of affairs regarding the other divisions.

It seemed that the Indian's mission had been a needless one, for Major Rogers's scouts had advised the same plan of advance which Sewatis spoke of, and he found them on the west bank of the creek, approaching our encampment with reasonable rapidity.

I questioned him regarding what he had seen of the enemy, and his reply was not reassuring.

It is true they yet remained some distance away, as if with no intention of advancing; but when we pressed Sewatis for his opinion, he gave it much as I have already stated: that the crafty savage was only biding his time when he could meet all three of the divisions, and he evidently had no doubt as to the final result.

I know that in saying this I am giving to that murderous villain a character different from that which he had borne up to that moment.

It was seldom his custom to attack large bodies of white men, but rather to wait until it should be possible to cut them off by detachments, thereby incurring less danger to his own precious person; but in this instance he was leading French soldiers as well as red brutes, and most likely counted upon impressing the frog-eaters with his skill in military tactics.

Perhaps I simply waste time in trying to make any explanation for the better understanding of that which followed; but yet it seems to me necessary, because all which occurred was so entirely different from what those who professed to be familiar with Indian warfare had ever experienced.

However, certain it is that Molang made no attempt at murdering Israel Putnam's little band, which he could easily have done offhand, and the other two divisions were allowed to join us unmolested.

I say "allowed," because we all in that encampment believed Molang was thoroughly well informed of the movements of each division.

Not until the following afternoon did the remainder of our force arrive, and then, as I heard one of the Rangers say, the corps numbered about five hundred, counting

English, Provincials, Rangers, and such few Indians as we had with us.

Sewatis was on the scout during this afternoon, and when he came in told Amos and I quite privately that Molang's crew were working up towards us.

The wily savage, now that we were together, most likely counted on making one job of it, and believed that he would be able to destroy us all.

During the last night at this encampment Israel Putnam moved to and fro as we had seen him at South Bay, and Amos said to me, when he passed for at least the tenth time where we were lying:

"The major has got the scent of the savages. When he walks about in that restless manner you may be certain danger is nigh."

We slept but little during this night, my comrade and I, and talked much to Sewatis, who felt confident we would soon be attacked.

The hour before daybreak is the one the red fiends most fancy, and when that time drew near at hand every Ranger and Provincial was on his feet.

It seemed strange to us that no sound was heard as the moments passed.

So profound was the silence that one almost feared to break it by even so much as a whisper, and those who were incredulous regarding Molang's force, such as Major Rogers and some of the British officers, came nigh to calling Israel Putnam a coward for taking so many precautions.

When the day dawned, we were still on the alert, and as yet undisturbed; but the most experienced woodsmen among us declared that we should not long be left in peace.

It had been decided among the leaders of the corps on the previous evening, as we learned from rumours which went about the camp, that, providing no hostile demonstration was made by Molang, we should start for Fort Edward at sunrise, and the time was near at hand.

Israel Putnam and Captain Dalyell wore an air of anxious expectancy.

Major Rogers was in the highest glee; to his mind the peril had been overrated, and the march to Fort Edward would cause no more than weariness.

Amos and I were watching him, believing it was in his mind to call Israel Putnam a coward in plain words, and to my thinking he did so when, from pure bravado, he challenged one of the red-coated lieutenants to shoot with him at a target.

During the fifteen or twenty minutes while we were preparing for the march did these two thus occupy themselves, and if Molang was not already well informed of our whereabouts, the reports of the firearms would speedily have warned him.

Then came the command to move, and Rogers's division marched in advance.

Our camping-place was surrounded by a dense thicket, beyond which was an open wood, therefore we who brought up the rear had little knowledge of what the foremost men were doing.

We could see file after file disappear among the tangled underbrush, and when, as might be supposed, the first division was well out of the thicket, there came a crash such as could not have been produced by less than fifteen hundred or two thousand muskets, and we knew that Molang was well satisfied with our position.

"Keep well together, boys, until we are out of this tangle!" Israel Putnam cried, and Amos said in a low tone to me:

"Our force of five or six hundred will be as nothing compared to those who are opposing us."

I believed the moment was near at hand when that "last bullet" of which the dear lad had spoken would be needed.

It was as if no more than three minutes elapsed from the time the report of the firearms first rang out with such volume, when, through the foliage, I caught sight of Major Rogers leading his division in retreat.

He had been incredulous as to the whereabouts of the enemy, and now evidently doubted his own courage.

"Stand steady, boys!" Israel Putnam said, hardly louder than a whisper, but so clearly that every one of us heard the words distinctly. "Stand steady, boys! All the more need of proving our metal if there be others who are faint-hearted."

That portion of the corps led by Captain Dalyell and Israel Putnam advanced to do battle as valiantly as though confident of success, and then was come the time when I have no clear idea of what I did.

When it was over, and we safe at Fort Edward once more, Amos also confessed to the same partial unconsciousness.

Like one in a dream I saw, after we were marched from the thicket into the open wood, the flash of weapons here and there, everywhere before me, like fireflies in a swamp; the report of musketry was as the crackling of a rattle incessantly whirled, and on every hand, as it seemed, were men dead or dying.

More than once did I dimly see a Ranger grapple with a painted savage, and, not thinking that I myself was in danger, I would stand in open-mouthed curiosity, wondering which of the two would rise from that deadly embrace.

Nearer and nearer came the Indians, --- the French we saw not.

The King's troops, for the greater part disregarding the opportunities for concealment behind the trees, stood their ground like men, until they were shot down or tomahawked.

How many were dragged away prisoners, later to be tortured with such cruelty as only these painted fiends can devise, no one may say; but again and again did I see half a dozen or more of the bloodthirsty wretches spring upon a soldier when his musket was empty and drag him to the ground, inflicting no injuries, lest by some mischance they kill him outright.

Then it was, and I know not how long a time after the

battle first opened, when it seemed as if our Rangers were in the very press of the conflict.

Israel Putnam no longer waved his sword to cheer us, but had taken a musket from the nerveless hands of its owner, and was using it with deadly precision perhaps not twenty paces in advance of where Amos and I stood sheltered by a pine-tree, the bark of which was cut and slashed as if by a hundred bullets.

Not more than twenty feet in front of him, each painted body sheltered, was the foremost line of Molang's crew, and our major, hoping, most like, to force them back and thereby revive the drooping spirits of Rogers's division, only a portion of which had come to our aid, sprang yet nearer the foe, urging us to follow him.

In trying to obey this command, Amos and I at the same instant left our shelter, and made for another tree a dozen paces or more in advance, at the very moment when the largest savage I ever saw sprang towards our major.

Putnam's musket was levelled, and, turning from thought of my own danger, I looked to see the Indian fall; but instead, our major's weapon misfired, and with the agility of a cat the half-naked brute leaped upon him, bearing him down.

We who witnessed this scene did not dare fire upon the enemy, lest we should kill him whom we would save, and the wretch understood full well what advantage was his.

As if with the sole desire to madden us, instead of carrying his prisoner to the rear, the Indian bound Israel Putnam hand and foot to a tree directly in front of their line, and instantly a dozen or more of the red fiends took up their station behind the helpless officer, firing at us, while we dared not return it.

"Unless we can save him, I hope a chance bullet may end our major's life," Amos Cowden said between his clenched teeth, and I came near to echoing the wish, remembering Robert Litchfield's fate.

Captain Dalyell did all an officer could do to free the prisoner.

Again and again was our little force mustered at one point, with due regard to sheltering ourselves, however, and the hottest fire was poured in close around where Israel Putnam was thus held helpless, with the hope that we might force back the savages; but all in vain.

Molang's crew knew only too well the advantage they thus had in making of our major a shield for their worthless bodies, and, as I have been told later, during more than an hour we fought manfully, desperately, without causing them to retreat so much as a yard.

Then it was we saw the same savage who had captured him come up from behind, taking good care not to expose his paint-begrimed carcass to our aim, and unloose the prisoner from the tree, keeping his arms and feet bound.

With one quick twist he pulled our major over his shoulder, and with a laugh of derision plunged further into the forest, until they were lost to view in the distance.

No one could fire without danger of killing our commander, and we were thus forced to see him borne away while we stood helplessly by.

Captain Dalyell was a brave man, and when Israel Putnam had been made captive, assumed command of the forces, for Rogers was skulking in the rear somewhere, and every one of us, although fighting desperately before, was nerved to yet greater exertions, in the faint hope that we might save our neighbour from Pomfret.

Later I heard it said that the capture of Israel Putnam gained for us the day, because every man, except those cowards in the rear, fought yet more bravely, thinking it might be possible to wrest from Molang's crew the prize they had taken.

As for Amos and myself, I only know, that for the time being, we forgot our lives were imperilled, in the thought of succouring him who was a friend as well as a commander, and after a time we were joined by Sewatis, who came from I know not where, but who fought like a demon.

The easy victory, which that brute Molang had expected, was not gained.

Step by step we advanced as the savage crew retreated. When our weapons were fouled with much using, we dropped them, exchanging with a dead man, or one so grievously wounded as to be unable to protect himself, and in such wise did the time pass until the fire from our front slackened, decreasing rapidly.

Then I heard some one shout:

"They are in retreat!"

We had won the day; but to my mind it would have been better had we lost the battle, and kept in our ranks that gallant gentleman from Pomfret.

Now that the danger was over, Major Rogers showed himself among the foremost, and I waited breathlessly, expecting to hear him order us forward in pursuit; but no such command was given.

We were standing, Amos and I, sheltered by a tree, as if the enemy were still seeking to take our lives, when there came to my ear a whisper in the Indian tongue:

"Are you of the mind to aid Major Putnam as you aided Sewatis?"

It was the Indian who spoke, and for reply I clasped him by the hand, Amos doing likewise; but hardly had assent thus been given, when I misdoubted our ability to accomplish anything amid so many.

"How may it be done, Sewatis?" I asked. "Surely we three cannot venture among Molang's forces, numerous as they are. What plan have you in mind?"

"What plan had you to save my life?"

"None whatever. We trusted to chance."

"And that is what we shall do now."

There seemed little hope. It was true Amos and I had succeeded in giving succour to Sewatis; but his captors numbered only eight, and Israel Putnam was held prisoner by all that remained alive of the two thousand or more whom Molang had led to battle.

The Indian would have set off at once; but I reminded him that both my comrade and myself were in need of ammunition, and we moved around among the dead and dying to get what store was necessary, seeing meanwhile such horrible sights as made my heart sick.

When we were done, and it can well be imagined there was no lingering amid such dreadful scenes, I turned to ask permission of Captain Dalyell, whom I looked upon as the next in command to Israel Putnam, even though Major Rogers was there. This last officer had proven himself a coward, and had no right to say what an honest man should or should not do.

"Where are you going?" Sewatis asked, quickly.

"To tell of our purpose."

"And for what reason? If you are denied permission?"

"I think in that case I should go at all hazards."

"We are soldiers," Amos interrupted, "even though we know not the manual of arms according to military training, and should we act in opposition to the commands of our officers, it would be a serious matter."

"Better go without speaking," Sewatis said, sharply. "If we are not found, it will be believed Molang's braves have taken us, and no one can be blamed."

The Indian was right. If we left the field at once no one could say we had gone without permission, — in fact, that which he suggested would be believed, and while I had little faith we could aid Israel Putnam, I was burning to make the attempt.

"Move around to the right, that we may not be observed, and once we are out of sight you shall say what is to be done."

This was Amos's method of settling matters, and I agreed to it by setting off as he had suggested.

Where every man was intent upon attending to those who were suffering, or yet guarding against a possible return of the enemy, it was a simple matter for us to leave without observation, and no more than ten minutes had elapsed from the time Molang's crew were in full retreat, before we pursued, on the wild chance of rescuing the prisoner who would be guarded more closely than any other, because of his rank.

CHAPTER VI.

THE PRISONER.

AMOS and I knew full well to what danger we were exposing ourselves in thus following the retreating savages.

Molang's force was so great that it hardly seemed probable his bloodthirsty wretches were disheartened by the drubbing they had received, and should it be discovered that we were so bold as to follow, every effort would be made to effect our capture.

Of course Sewatis knew this as well as we, but such work was his trade, so to speak, and he would have made the venture even though the stake was not so high.

Do not suppose that either Amos or I were growing timorous after we set out.

Such feeling had come upon me, at least, before we started, and although I had little hope we could effect anything, there was no thought of turning back.

Of one thing we were certain: no better leader could have been found, and so long as we obeyed his orders, unless the fates were desperately against us, there was good reason for believing we might hold our own.

As proof that the savages were not in a panic of fear, we caught glimpses, now and then, of the hindermost, before half an hour had passed, and when we arrived at a certain dense thicket where were so many thorns that there was little chance Molang's half-naked villains would venture, save they knew their prey was concealed within, Sewatis called a halt.

"We will rest here," he said, speaking as quietly as though we had been out for a day's hunting, and were weary. "We will rest here; the major is in no danger until nightfall, and there is fear we may by chance come upon the laggards in the flight, which would be unpleasant."

All this he spoke in the Indian tongue, and I must add in favour of Sewatis, whom Amos and I had known many a year, he never used those high-sounding words which I have since heard people say the Indians indulge in.

For my part, all of the redskins whom I have seen and heard speak in their own language, talk much as do we, with precious little about the "Great Spirit," "Happy Hunting Grounds," or other folderol which is oftentimes put in their mouths by those who never had the ill-fortune to meet them.

Amos and I were not loath to do as Sewatis proposed, and knew the hiding-place would be a safe one for a certain time at least, because of the difficulty we had in entering the thicket without cutting our flesh by the thorns.

Here until the day was well-nigh spent did we remain, and, although it may seem strange after all the dreadful scenes we had witnessed, both Amos and I spent a goodly portion of the time in slumber.

It was well that we did so, since it might be the last chance for many a long hour.

When the sun was no more than an hour high, and after we had seen well to the priming of our muskets, as well as made certain everything we carried was in its proper place, the pursuit was resumed.

I have seen much trailing, both before the battle on Clear River and since, but never such skilful work as was done by the Indian Sewatis on this day, so long as it was light enough to read the signs on the ground.

Although many Indians had passed, and among them no less than three hundred Frenchmen, he would point now and then to what he insisted was the mark of Israel Putnam's boots; and I have no question but that he was in the right, for when, two hours after sunset, we came upon where Molang's murderers were encamped, there was no need to search for the prisoner.

He was there, and we could not have followed more directly had we walked in full view of him as he was forced through the woods by his merciless captors.

The camp-fires everywhere around told that the savages were not fearful of pursuit. They knew only too well how few in numbers was the force they had attacked, and understood, or believed they did, that no attempt would be made to renew the battle.

Had Captain Dalyell followed us with a hundred men, that band of murderers might have been considerably reduced, for not a sentinel was stationed, as far as we could make out, anywhere around the encampment, and a surprise would have been disastrous while they were busy in their barbarous work of torturing prisoners.

Because of the many camp-fires we could see our poor major plainly, and the sight was a woeful one.

Stripped naked, he was bound fast to a sapling in the very centre of the encampment, and half a dozen or more wretches were busily engaged piling dry wood around the base of the tree.

We knew only too well what all this meant, and Amos clutched my hand until his grasp was painful, as from behind the shelter we looked on at these preparations.

We had come to within a hundred yards of the outermost line of fires, where any one of the crew might stumble upon us by chance, and yet, because of that scene before us, heeded not the danger.

"They are going to burn him," Amos whispered in my ear, and I strove hard to keep the tears from my eyes as I nodded in assent.

"Are we to do nothing?" he asked, a moment later, and a fierce anger came upon me as I replied:

"The most we could do now would be to die with him. What may three avail here, where are no less than five hundred?"

I might have set the number twice that, and not been wrong, for the encampment was a large one, showing that here was the bulk of Molang's men.

Sewatis gazed at the scene in silence, watching every

detail, and so great was my rage because of our helplessness that I could not forbear saying in his ear :

"We are come as you wished. Now what may it be possible to do?"

"I hoped for some chance such as came to you when I, like him, was near to death, but it is denied us."

"And we have come here for no other purpose than to see him die."

"That would please him, could he know it. When I stood as does he, and saw you, my heart grew lighter, even though at the time I did not believe you could stay the fire, or ward off death by so much as a moment."

Yes, we were come before he died; but he would not know it, and we should suffer at least a portion of the torture which must be his, in witnessing the horrible scene.

As the bloodthirsty wretches piled the wood around him with infinite care, my rage grew so great that, if Sewatis had proposed for us three to rush in and kill as many of the brutes as we could, I would have gladly agreed, without thinking of what must follow such a mad venture.

Presently all was done as these scoundrels would have it, and I saw more than one French officer, who would have considered himself insulted had he been accused of being a savage, walk curiously up to look at the unfortunate major, or examine the arrangements for his death.

Then the brutes began to gather nearabout the stake,

and we knew that Israel Putnam's time of torture was near at hand.

There was much shouting, dancing, discharging of firearms, and brandishing of tomahawks and knives, as if certain ceremonies were being gone through with, after which the huge savage who had captured our major advanced, and set fire to the light wood.

Save that the flames had been burning into my flesh instead of his, I do not think it would be possible for me to have suffered more than I did while viewing this horrible spectacle.

It was with difficulty I could keep myself from shrieking, and Amos clasped my wrist until it was as if a cord had been wound tightly around it.

Sewatis remained silent. To have judged simply from the expression on his face, one would have said he was indifferent to the scene.

Again I asked, hardly knowing what I did, if it was not possible for us to strike one blow in the defence of our friend, and again the Indian shook his head.

We knew beyond a peradventure that no assistance could come from those troops we had left behind us, and I was positive that, when another sun should set, the gallant gentleman from Pomfret would be no longer of this world.

I prayed fervently that some brute, while brandishing his knife or tomahawk, might inadvertently strike the fatal blow, and thus relieve the unhappy prisoner from his sufferings.

Higher and higher the flames mounted. Our major was doing his best to repress any show of suffering, and yet we saw him move his head this way or that as if to escape the torture of the flames.

It was while this orgy was at its height, while I was praying death might come speedily, that a drop of water fell upon my face.

Glancing upward quickly, I saw a storm-cloud in the sky, and it was as if I had but just looked when there came a downpour of rain like unto a flood.

The cruel flames were beaten out.

The prisoner raised his face so far as was possible to receive this unexpected aid from heaven, and I could well fancy how refreshing was the splash of the drops upon his blistered skin.

It seemed as if he had been saved because of my prayer, and I was nigh to crying aloud with joy, when the horrible thought came that this sudden downpour of water would but prolong his agony.

The bloodthirsty wretches, once the rain had ceased falling, would ignite the pile again, and he was simply respited for so long a time as the shower should continue.

"He is saved! He is saved!" Amos cried, heeding not that by such exclamation he might be revealing our presence to the foe.

Sewatis shook his head. For the first time since this fiendish orgy had begun did he speak:

"It is only for a time," he said. "Better the rain had not fallen, for he would be so much nearer the end."

While the shower lasted, say, perhaps, ten minutes, the murdering crew stood silent and motionless around the stake, and as the clouds passed away they recommenced the orgy.

I looked to see them rekindle the fire, but, apparently, no one gave heed to it, and once more Amos said, hopefully:

"They are not going to burn him. Perhaps, having seen that heaven has interposed in the dreadful work, they will content themselves with such antics as are now going on."

"They content themselves with knowing that the embers will soon be fanned into a blaze," Sewatis said; and now it was we could see tiny sparks of fire here and there, which were gradually growing larger.

Although the flames on the top of the pile had been beaten out by the rain, there was sufficient light wood beneath yet burning to rekindle the whole.

Even as we watched, and before there was time to speak, first one yellow tongue and then another leaped up, until once more the gentleman from Pomfret was encircled by the fiery element.

Again I prayed that death might come quickly, and again was it shown to me how little we understand what it is best to ask.

When the blaze was fiercest, and just as it seemed to me that with each indrawing of the unfortunate man's breath he was bringing death so much the nearer, a figure, in the uniform of a French officer, dashed through the howling, maddened throng, kicked the embers aside as if in a rage, and, as soon as might be, severed the prisoner's bonds.

"Some Frenchman is proving that he is not quite a savage," Amos muttered, and Sewatis turned, as if our work was done here, while he replied:

"It is Molang himself. He wears the uniform of those whose ally he prides himself on being. The prisoner will not suffer death."

"Not suffer death!" I repeated. "Has Molang suddenly repented of his ways?"

"I know not how that may be, but certain it is that Major Putnam's life has been saved. He will now be carried a prisoner to Canada."

"How do you know but that they will lead him to the stake again?" Amos asked, incredulously.

"Not after his life has been spared by the chief. He is as safe as any prisoner in their hands can be, and we may return to Fort Edward."

Sewatis gave us no opportunity of questioning him further; but turning, walked swiftly away in the direction from which we had come, trusting that, during the confusion consequent upon this interruption of the torture, we might pass unheeded.

Not until we were two miles or more away did the Indian halt, and, as if to excuse himself, made the following explanation :

"Molang having interfered when the prisoner was at the stake, there could be no further question of Major Putnam's ever being subjected to a like torture, and no reason now, if indeed there was any half an hour previous, why we should linger in that locality."

In fact, it was wisest we depart then, for, after the cruel sport had thus come to an end, the howling brutes might take it into their heads to make certain they were not followed by the British forces.

"But if he is still held a prisoner, we have not accomplished or even attempted to accomplish, that for which we came," Amos said, when, the explanation concluded, Sewatis resumed the march.

"I did not believe we could set him free unless by some chance, and it was hardly likely that would come. There is no possibility now."

"But yet you were eager to set out with the hope of aiding him?"

"I had little belief of being able to do that. It was my purpose, at the last moment, when he could yet understand what was being done, to avenge his death, and perish with him."

"Did you count on our doing the same?" Amos asked, in a tone of horror.

"No; but I wanted you to see it, so that in time to come, if any of Molang's tribe fell into your power, you could taunt them with having lost so many of their braves for the sake of torturing one white man. Now we will go back, and quickly, for every musket will be needed at Fort Edward once the French soldiers have recovered from their alarm."

From that moment, until we arrived at the fort, no halt was made.

I tell you this story, lad, to show how we fought in 1758, and there is no reason why I should continue to speak of what Amos Cowden and I may have done when we served the King, and Israel Putnam languished in a French prison at Montreal.

You already know of his distressing march from that encampment, where he came so near his death, to Ticonderoga, and thence to Canada. Also, of how he was released, and, unless I mistake not, you can tell with greater detail of what he did when he served the colonists, than when he served the King.

THE END.

www.ingramcontent.com/pod-product-compliance
Lightning Source LLC
Chambersburg PA
CBHW031409160426
43196CB00007B/959